30 OCTOBER 2008

TERRORISM, INSURGENCY OR FREEDOM STRUGGLE

CORNEL GENERAL

Contents

Contents

CHAPTER I

Introduction

The year 2008 has seen terrorist attacks in Jaipur, Bangalore, Ahmedabad, New Delhi, Agartala, Imphal andAssam. The month of October alone witnessed terrorist attacks in Tripura and Manipur, before the October 30 serial bomb blasts in Assam. On 1 October 2008, four explosions in Agartala left two civilians dead and nearly 100 injured, while the blasts in Imphal on October 21 killed 18 civilians. The 9 serial blasts in Assam on October 30 killed 83 civilians and injured more than 300. The pattern of these terrorist attacks seems to indicate a seamless web of connection among terrorist outfits across the length and breadth of the country. Similarities between the bomb blasts are striking: public places especially market areas have been targeted aimed at causing civilian deaths. The Assam blasts had an added brutality: the use of car bombs packed with RDX and ammonium nitrate. The blasts in other cities like Jaipur, Ahmedabad or New Delhi earlier were of a lower intensity.

In the immediate aftermath of the blasts, a hitherto unknown outfit calling itself Islamic Security Force (Indian Mujahideen) or ISF (IM) was held responsible for the blasts by the Assam Police based on an SMS it supposedly sent to a Guwahati based television news channel News Live, claiming responsibility for this dastardly act. Incidentally, the Islamic Security Force, without any link to the Indian Mujahideen, was formed in 2000 during the Bodo separatist movement with the aim of protecting the interests of Muslim migrant settlers in the Bodo dominated district of

1

Kokrajhar. However, no evidence of terror activities by the ISF had come to light before October 30. It may be possible that the ISF has begun to collaborate with the Indian Mujahideen – responsible for the terrorist attacks in Jaipur, Ahmedabad and New Delhi. It must be noted that the authenticity of the SMS has since been questioned and the Assam Police has subsequently stated that it could be a "hoax" aimed at misleading investigations.

The Security Forces have also asserted that the United Liberation Front of Asom (ULFA) and the Harkat-ul-Jehadi-e-Islami (HuJI) joined forces to carry out the Assam blasts. But ULFA has denied any involvement in the blasts. The HuJI's involvement has been inferred from the use of RDX. Security Forces also argue that since ULFA is a discredited force in Assam the outfit might want to terrorize people into supporting its so-called cause of Independent Sovereign Asom. This is, however, a highly unlikely proposition. ULFA had learnt its lessons after its 2004 indiscriminate bomb blasts at Dhemaji district which killed 10 school children and seven others. The public outcry against the outfit at that time resulted in diminished ULFA influence. Hence, ULFA would avoid targeting the ethnic group it claims to represent for fear of a fresh public outcry against the outfit. Also, ULFA has no base in Kokrajhar, and thus it is not easy for it to carry out blasts there. Logically too, the outfit would avoid from being openly seen as collaborating with HuJI in carrying out deadly terrorist attacks in ethnic Assamese inhabited areas, for this would further alienate the outfit from its already limited support base.

Fresh evidence put forth by the Assam Police now suggests that the National Democratic Front of Bodoland (NDFB) engineered the attacks based on orders issued by its founder and chief, Rajan Daimary, in September 2008. The attacks are seen as a kind of "signalling" to communicate the NDFB's growing frustration of at the lack of progress in its talks with the Union government. The police further assert that ULFA provided the infrastructural backup to the NDFB to carry out the attacks, and that ULFA military chief Paresh Barua, who is based in Bangladesh, was desperate to showcase his outfit's lethality against the backdrop of its sagging reputation in Assam.

It is too early to pass a conclusive verdict on the identity of the perpetrators of October 30 terrorist attacks given the multiple theories being floated by the security agencies. However, each of the three outfits mentioned so far have motives to carry out these attacks. A major aim could be to terrorize a particular population base – ethnic Assamese or Bodo in the case of ISF (IM), Assamese in the case of ULFA and Assamese as well as Bodos in the case of the NDFB. The blasts could also have been an act of coercive intimidation and response by either the ISF (IM) or the NDFB to the recent ethnic violence between ethnic Bodos and immigrant Muslim settlers in Darrang and Uddalguri, which led to the death of 60 people and the displacement of more than 100,000 people. Another motive could be to destabilise Assam at the behest of external intelligence agencies like Pakistan's Inter-Service Intelligence (ISI) and the Directorate of Field Intelligence (DGFI) of Bangladesh.

As usual, various arms of the government have begun to blame each other for failure to prevent the terrorist attacks. The Army claims that it had warned the Assam government on several occasions of impending terrorist attacks being planned by the ULFA and HuJI. The Union Home Ministry had also warned the Assam government of an impending terror attack. But the state government blames the lack of actionable intelligence from the Army. Significantly, the claim of responsibility by the ISF (IM) or the recent police claims about the involvement of the NDFB further complicates the situation as the needle of suspicion is shifted from the ULFA and HuJI to two other outfits about whose activities the Army's warnings had been silent about. This also absolves the Assam government from charges of complacency. Nonetheless, what is disturbing is the unpreparedness of the state machinery to handle the situation. The security forces are not equipped to handle the immediate post-blasts phase. Personnel of both security forces and the fire brigade failed to reach the affected locales in time.

One commonly held point in Assam and elsewhere is that Bangladesh-based anti-India forces are actively indulging in terrorist activities from across the international border. This has also been highlighted by high level police and paramilitary officials. A porous border, continued illegal immigration, nexus between Bangladesh-based terror outfits and extra regional forces with local militant groups and arms trafficking across the border, all make terrorist attacks like the October 30 serial blasts possible. But policy makers often tend to ignore the harsh realities of an ethnically volatile region and adopt an ad hoc strategy without a deeper understanding of the social and political contradictions existing on the ground. Even after 23 years of the signing of the Assam Accord, the fence along the India-Bangladesh border has not been completed. Both the Central and state governments have failed to check the flow of illegal migrants, upgrade the National Registrar of Citizens (NRC), arrest arms traffickersand deal with armed movements. Instead, security forces have engaged in counter-insurgency operations without addressing the root causes of armed conflicts and countering external linkages.

India has also been unable to sustain a dialogue mechanism with Bangladesh for resolution of the issue of illegal migrants. Till date, about 12 lakh Bangladeshi nationals have entered India legally with visa but have subsequently vanished without trace. This reflects the inability on the part of law enforcing agencies to perform the tasks of detecting and deporting these Bangladeshi citizens. If this is the state of affairs with regard to legal migrants, how can these agencies handle the flow of illegal migrants? The more worrying implication of this illegal flow of migrants in Assam is that local Muslims are being looked upon with suspicion by the other indigenous communities. Unless the core issues are settled and the root causes addressed through a well formulated strategy and with political conviction, bringing stability to this part of India is not going to be easy.

CHAPTER II

2008 Assam bombings

The **2008 Assam bombings** occurred on 30 October 2008, before noon in markets in Guwahati city and the surrounding area of western Assam. Reports indicated as many as eighteen bombs went off, causing at least 81 deaths and 470 injuries.

Union Minister Shakeel Ahmed confirmed 10 blasts took place, however reports did indicate the number could have been as high as eighteen. The blasts ripped apart Guwahati, Barpeta Road, Bongaigaon and Kokrajhar.

The explosions in Guwahati ripped through Pan Bazar, Fancy Bazar and Ganeshguri, which were crowded with shoppers and office goers. Three blasts occurred in Kokrajhar, with another possible grenade explosion, one in Bongaigaon and two in Barpeta Road. Indian media outlets pointed out that the blasts took place just after the *Diwali* holidays making the blasts even more unexpected and adding to a toll count. The bomb at Ganeshguri was planted in a car and took place about 100 meters from Chief Minister of Assam Tarun Gogoi's official residence.

In Guwahati, 41 people were killed, in Kokrajhar, 21 and in Barpeta Road, 15. On 2 November 2008, four more succumbed to their injuries here. Three died at Gauhati Medical College Hospital, while another died at the Basistha Army Hospital. Twenty others were also in a critical condition.

Police officials added that huge amounts of explosives like <u>RDX</u> or other <u>plastic explosives</u>, like <u>C4</u>, have been used as a fire erupted immediately following the blasts. Timers were also speculated to have been used to execute the blasts, which were seen with timing almost to perfection as the blasts took place within a short span of 15 minutes. It was further speculated after investigations were initiated, that motorbikes may have been used. However, Assam police chief RN Mathur also said most of the bombs were "planted in cars." In addition to the immediate casualty toll seven more people succumbed to their injuries overnight.

CHAPTER III

Immediate consequences

- Immediately following the attack the <u>Government of Assam</u> issued a high alert and called out <u>paramilitary</u> forces to control a potentially volatile situation. Security was also increased in the <u>Jalpaiguri</u> district following the blasts. The police and <u>Sima Suraksha Bal</u> (<u>Border Security Force</u>) were said to be keeping a joint vigilance along the Bangladesh border. The superintendent of police, Jalpaiguri, Manoj Varma, said that police had been instructed to keep around the clock vigilance over important public places in the district.

- Following the blasts, angry crowds clashed with police in some areas of Guwahati. Some people were injured in the clash and at one point, police had to fire in the air to disperse an angry mob. It was also reported on the television media that mobs were hampering efforts by police and the fire brigade to clean up after the blasts. The mobs were seen attacking police and fire equipment. A <u>curfew</u> had been imposed in Guwahati and some other cities of Assam following the serial bomb blasts.

- It was also reported that members of the Assamese diaspora trying to contact relatives following the blasts faced jammed telephone networks, making it impossible to get information out of the region.

- <u>Gauhati Medical College and Hospital</u> where the victims are being treated have reported an acute shortage of blood. The Health Minister <u>HimantaBiswaSarmah</u> has urged the people to donate blood. <u>AsomGanaParishad</u> has directed the party cadres to donate blood. Several NGOs and volunteers of social organisations have come forward to <u>donate blood</u> and provide help to family members of the injured and those who have lost their lives.

- In response to the <u>TarunGogoi</u> government's alleged failure to protect Assam, a motley crowd attempted to storm into the state secretariat with two charred bodies from the blasts as hundreds more took to the streets in protest. The mob, shouting slogans like "*TarunGogoimurdabad*", was stopped at the gates of the seat of government by the security staff. They also demanded that "Gogoi come out and see what your failure to protect the people has caused. It has killed innocent people."

Follow up

On the same day a convoy of police cars in Assam came under fire from rebels resulting in seven police and three civilian casualties.

CHAPTER IV

Consequences

A spontaneous *bandh* total shut down, was observed the next day at Kokrajhar on a call given by the <u>Vishva Hindu Parishad</u> (VHP), the <u>Bharatiya Janata Party</u> (BJP)and the <u>Bajrang Dal</u>, while schools and educational institutions also remained closed in Guwahati. Only a few shops in the capital were opened and vehicular traffic was thin with most people choosing to stay indoors. BJP leader <u>L. K. Advani</u>, who arrived in Assam on the same morning, visited the blast site near the Deputy Commissioner's office, where he also faced a group of angry lawyers who shouted slogans saying "Advani go back." He also visited the <u>Gauhati Medical College and Hospital</u> and met the injured. The Union <u>Home MinisterShivrajPatil</u>, who was arrived later in the day, visited Kokrajhar and Barpeta. He also held a high-level meeting at the LokopriyoGopinathBordoloi International Airport in the evening. Attendance in commercial areas where offices are located was thin and in many areas shops and business establishments, particularly those in and around the blast sites remained closed. Few public transports were seen plying on the roads in the morning. The opposition <u>AsomGanaParishad</u> observed a *Black Day* with all its leaders and cadres sporting black badges. Lawyers from both Gauhati High Court and the Sessions Court in Guwahati abstained from work and held protests outside the court premises.

A curfew was again clamped on the worst-hit Ganeshguri in the afternoon after the initial curfew was relaxed the previous evening as an angry mob braved tight security in the presence of the city SS and went on a rampage. The police then resorted to firing blanks, injuring at least five people in the ensuing melee. The leader of the opposition and former Deputy Prime Minister Advani visited the spot just minutes before the disturbance.

On 1 November 2008, the prime minister was set to visit his home constituency to take the stock of the situation after the blasts. He would meet the Assam Governor Shiv CharanMathur and Chief Minister TarunGogoi, as well as visit the Gauhati Medical College and Hospital to see the injured in the blasts.

As a result of this blast, the biggest in Assamese history, CM Gogoi moved to recruit 4,000 more police personnel in all ranks to augment the strength of the police force to over 65,000 before the end of the year as part of Assam's counter-terrorism plan. He added the necessity of such a move was predicated by having experienced 605 bomb blasts in the last eight years, each of which caused significant devastation to life and property. He added that police and other security personnel had also recovered or defused more than 5,000 bombs and grenades.

CHAPTER V

Investigation

The Union home secretary, <u>Madhukar Gupta</u>, said a team of <u>National Security Guards</u> experts from New Delhi also visited the blast sites at Ganeshguri, the deputy commissioner's office and Fancy Bazaar. When asked about the nature of the explosives, he said forensic experts were already examining the blasts sites. In regards to more paramilitary forces, saying there were already enough forces deployed, he added: "We will retain them for some more time and probably not deploy them on poll duties (in six states)." A high-level team consisting of senior Home Ministry officials also visited Assam to make an on-the-spot assessment of the situation arising out blasts.

Police said they had picked up about a dozen suspects for interrogation within the first 24 hours. An official in the police department said: "We are making good headway in our investigations and should be able to zero in on the people or groups involved in the serial bombings." Two persons from Nagaon district were arrested in connection with the attacks. Asib Mohammed Nizami and Zulfikar Ali were the owners of two vehicles in which the bombs were planted in the Ganeshguri area of Guwahati and Bongaigaon.

On 1 November 2008, the army told the Prime Minister that it had previously intercepted a message from Calcutta one week before the incident that said: "Attack Guwahati." The army told the PM that had known about the impending terror strikes in the western Assam towns for six weeks and had tried to prevent them. Lt. Gen. B.S. Jaswal, of the GOC

4 Corps, told the PM the army had received "non-specific" information on 17 September 2008 about possible strikes in Guwahati, Barpeta Road and Kokrajhar. CM Gogoi, who heads Assam's unified command that includes the army, corroborated the message with Singh. In admitting such knowledge he added that the government did not anticipate the scale of the blasts. The government then also formed a special team, headed by the inspector-general of police (special task force), R. Chandranathan, to probe the blasts and issue a report within 30 days.

Evidence emerged that a hit-team of the National Democratic Front of Bodoland (NDFB) executed the bombings in Assam. This undermined earlier claims of HuJI responsibility. Police were quoted as saying a text message sent to a local television station claiming responsibility for the bombings on behalf of the hitherto unknown Islamic Security Force-Indian Mujahideen turned out to be a hoax. Assam police investigators determined that two of the three Maruti 800s used as bombs were purchased by NDFB activists less than six weeks before the attacks. Interrogation of suspects linked to the fabrication of the car-bombs led investigators to believe that there were orders to initiate the operation by the NDFB founder-chief, RanjanDaimary, as early as September 2008. Daimary, believed to shuttle between Bangkok, Manila and Singapore is said to have authorised the attacks to signal frustration with the lack of progress in talks between the NDFB and the Indian government.

Following this, the Indian government decided to clamp down on the organization and other regional outfits. A ban on the NDFB, set to expire in 2008 was extended by two years. The Cabinet Committee on Security also decided to re-impose a ban on the outlawed ULFA and Hynniewtrep

National Liberation Council (HNLC), however it spared the ANVC.

On 12 November 2008, a Bhutanese man who lived in Nepal and fought against the monarchy was arrested for aiding the Assam attacks. Tenzing G. Zangpo, a senior leader of the Druk National Congress (DNC), a formation by Bhutanese exiles in Nepal was picked up with the "home secretary" of the NDFB Sabin Boro from a rented house at Japorigog in Guwahati. An unknown source was quoted as saying, "After interrogation, both of them were arrested this morning on the charge of being part of the conspiracy behind October 30 blasts." The arrest attention from Bangladesh based forces to Bhutan for the first time since the probe was initiated. Police said the DNC claimed to be a political outfit opposing the alleged discrimination of Bhutanese people of Nepali origin by the monarchy since the 1990s.

CHAPTER VI

Perpetrators

Union Minister Shakil Ahmed hinted that communal riots in Assam for the preceding several days could be inter-linked to the attacks. He said that the politics of hate was a plausible reason behind the attacks.

Fresh evidence put forth by the Assam Police now suggests that the National Democratic Front of Bodoland (NDFB) engineered the attacks based on orders issued by its founder and chief, RajanDaimary in September 2008.

CHAPTER VII

Central reactions

Leader of the opposition L. K. Advani used the blasts to lambaste the ruling UPA-led government. He said: "I believe that these blasts are symbolic of the sense of insecurity in the country. This also proves the total failure of the government in combating terrorism", adding that it was likely that illegal Bangladeshi migrants in Assamwith an increasing influx of such immigrantscould be involved in the blasts.

The next day he came out again blaming illegal infiltration from Bangladesh as the main reason for the breeding of terrorism in Assam saying "I blame the state and the central government for the blasts in Assam." He continued to question the PM, "I ask the prime minister, who is elected from Assam, what his government has done after the Supreme Court's landmark judgment on the IMDT (Illegal Migrants Determination by Tribunals) Act indicating the Government of India for having colluded with external aggression. The government only incorporated all those provisions in the struck down IMDT in the Foreigners Act, which the Supreme Court declared as unconstitutional." He also visited blast sites and met injured victims at the hospitals.

Union Minister of State for Home, ShriprakashJaiswal, also condemned the blasts and added: "The blasts will have no impact on the forthcoming Assembly elections in Mizoram. The Home Ministry has asked for a report on the serial blasts from the Assam government." He claimed that due to the sincere efforts of the ruling central coalition government, incidents of terror in the northeastern sister states had gone down by as much as 50 per cent in the last four years.

The prime minister also strongly condemning the blasts and added that his government would take all possible steps to bring the perpetrators of the attack to justice.Along with the UPA chairperson, Sonia Gandhi, were set to visit Assam on 1 November 2008. The day before Union Home Minister, Shivraj Patil, also arrived in Assam and visited blast sites in Kokrajhar and Guwahati, as well as holding a security meeting with the chief minister and senior police and administrative officials. He said: "We shall nab the culprits involved in the blasts. Investigations are on and we should be able to come out with something concrete."

Former Indian prime minister Atal Behari Vajpayee hinted at a call for greater national unity and what he termed a collective war on terror after the blasts.

CHAPTER VIII

Pan-Indian reactions

The Jharkhand government also came out strongly condemning the serial blasts, while having summoned a cabinet meeting in Ranchi for the next day to discuss the security situation in his region. Deputy Chief Minister, Sudhir Mahto, described the act as one of "cowardice" and said the state machinery had been alerted in Jharkhand following the incident. He added that he expressed confidence that the UPA government at the centre would initiate all necessary steps to rein in anti-national elements who are bent upon weakening the prevailing peace and tranquillity, while appealing to the central government to provide adequate compensation to the family members of the victims. While he also denied the fact that the militant activities were on the rise in the country at large during the rule of the UPA government, he expressed concern over the recent revelation that Hindu militants' were involved in the Malegaon incident. He said this by alluding to the fact that vested interests were keen on dividing the country by creating panic.Vigilance was also stepped up along the West Bengal border with Assam following the blasts. Additional security forces were rushed to assist in combing operations to track down those responsible for the blasts attempting to flee from Assam through the border with North Bengal. State's Home Secretary, Ashok Mohan Chakavarty, said an alert had been sounded across West Bengal, with security tightened in the capital city. Further security arrangements were under review, particularly in the border districts where check-posts have been set up. A senior police official in West Bengal said: "A special alert has been sounded in the region. Vehicles passing through the border with Assam are being checked." He added that surveillance had also been considerably tightened at West Bengal's international borders with Nepal, Bangladesh and Bhutan.

Uttar Pradesh Chief Minister, Mayawati, also strongly condemned the serial blasts, while demanding that the Prime Minister take effective measures to ensure that such incidents are not repeated.

CHAPTER IX

International reactions

U.N. Secretary-General <u>Ban Ki-moon</u>, who was in India at the time of the attack, issued a statement via a spokesman expressing his deep sorrow and sympathy to the government and people of India for the loss of life and destruction caused by the attacks. He also stated that he "strongly condemns this act of terrorism in its targeting of civilians", also declaring that there can be no justification for such indiscriminate violence.

<u>Russian PresidentDmitry Medvedev</u> resolutely condemned the deadly blasts dubbing them as an "inhuman and monstrous" crime which cannot have any justification. In a message to <u>Indian PresidentPratibhaPatil</u> and Prime Minister Singh, he expressed his indignation at the "barbarous" act and called for strict punishment for those responsible. He said: "I learnt with deep indignation about the series of coordinated terrorist acts in Assam, which led to the deaths of scores of innocent people. Such inhuman and monstrous in cruelty crime have no justification. Terrorists guilty of committing this barbarous act must be severely punished." The <u>Russian Foreign Ministry</u> also said: "The Foreign Ministry of Russia resolutely condemns the acts of terrorists. They have no and cannot have any justification. The criminals must be severely punished for their acts."

Bangladesh also strongly condemned the attack. Foreign adviser <u>Iftekhar Ahmed Chowdhury</u> term the attack an act of "cowardly terrorism." Adding: "We strongly condemn the bomb blast in the North-Eastern India that led to so many deaths and injuries. It is a cowardly act of terrorism. Violence cannot be a tool for the achievement of political objectives."

CHAPTER X

National Democratic Front of Bodoland (NDFB)

The National Democratic Front of Boroland (NDFB) was an armed separatist outfit which sought to obtain a sovereign Boroland for the Bodo people. It is designated as a terrorist organisation by the Government of India. But since there is no universally accepted definition of terrorism, its very hard to define who is a terrorist. NDFB according to itself is a revolutionary organisation struggling for a free and independent Boroland.

NDFB traces its origin to Bodo Security Force(BSF), an insurgent group formed in 1986. The current name was adopted in 1994, after the group rejected Bodo Accord signed between the Government of India and ABSU-BPAC. After 1996, NDFB was also involved in conflicts with the militant group Bodo Liberation Tigers Force (which surrendered in 2003). Since 2000, NDFB has increasingly targeted illegal Bangladeshi immigrants in what it claims to be the Boro territory.

During the 1990s, NDFB established 12 camps on the Bhutan-Assam border. After suffering major reverses during Royal Bhutan Army's Operation All Clear, NDFB signed a ceasefire with the Indian authorities in May 2005.

This was followed by a split in the group: NDFB (P), the progressive faction supported peace talks with the government, while the faction led by Nabla opposed the talks. In 2012, following the arrest of their chairman, NDFB of Nabla faction split further, leading to the formation of another new faction, which was led by a non-Bodo I. K. Songbijit as an interim president of the interim council.

The general assembly of the outfit held on 14 and 15 April 2015 vowed to revamp their national struggle and declared that the former interim national council of NDFB led by Songbijit is dissolved and a new national council was formed to fight for the liberation of sovereign, independent Boroland.

The NDFB signed a peace treaty with the government in 2020 and disbanded itself.

CHAPTER XI

Objectives

The main grievances of the group are the under-development in the region and the influx of immigrants. It aims to address these issues by seceding from India, and establishing a sovereign Boroland. The NDFB constitution, adopted on 10 March 1998, lists its objectives as the following:

- Liberate Boroland from the Indian expansionism and occupation;
- Free the Boro nation from the colonialist exploitation, oppression and domination;
- Establish a Democratic Socialist Society to promote Liberty, Equality and Fraternity; and
- Uphold the integrity and sovereignty of Boroland.

The promotion of the Roman script for the Bodo language is also a significant objective of NDFB and are against the use of Devanagari script for the language.

CHAPTER XII

History

The <u>Bodos</u> are an ethno-linguistic community native to the <u>Brahmaputra Valley</u> in Assam state of India. In the mid-1980s, Bodo politicians, alleging discrimination against Bodos in Assam, intensified their campaign for the creation of Bodo-majority <u>Bodoland</u>. While majority of the Bodos envisaged Bodoland as an autonomous territory or state within India, a small section demanded complete sovereignty. NDFB was formed by secessionist Bodos on 3 October 1986 as the Bodo Security Force (BdSF), under the leadership of <u>Ranjan Daimary</u>, in OdlaKhasibari village (near <u>Udalguri</u>).

The Bodoland movement was mainly led by the political organisations <u>All Bodo Students Union</u> (ABSU) and <u>Bodo Peoples' Action Committee</u> (BPAC). In 1993, these two groups signed the Bodo Accord with Indian government, agreeing to the formation of Bodoland Autonomous Council within Assam. BdSF opposed this Accord. Shortly after the Accord, the Assam State Government refused to hand over 2,750 villages to the proposed Council, arguing that Bodos formed less than 50% of the population in these villages. Following this, the BdSF was renamed to National Democratic Front of Bodoland (NDFB) on 25 November 1994.

In the mid-1990s, NDFB also faced a rival within the Bodo community, in form of <u>Bodo Liberation Tigers Force</u> (BLTF). The BLTF had evolved from an older militant group called the Bodo Volunteer Force. It considered NDFB's secessionist agenda unrealistic and unattainable, and focused on establishment of an autonomous Bodo territory within India. After 1996, the two groups clashed violently for supremacy. BLTF allied with Bengali Tiger Force, a terrorist of Bengali, to protect Bengali speaking immigrants and the immigrants are also supported by Indian security forces against NDFB. The conflicts between Christian-dominated NDFB and Hindu-dominated BLTF polarised the Bodoland movement along religious lines. In 2003, BLTF surrendered en masse in return for the establishment of the Bodoland Territorial Council.

NDFB had established 12 camps on the Bhutan-Assam border. During 2003-2004, the Royal Bhutan Army destroyed these camps as part of its Operation All Clear. NDFB chief Ranjan Daimary was offered amnesty by the Assam Chief Minister Tarun Gogoi in December 2003, but rejected the offer. On 8 October 2004, the NDFB announced a six-month-long unilateral ceasefire, that came into effect on 15 October. However, the Government continued its operations against the group. On 15 April 2005, NDFB extended the ceasefire. The Government released its general secretary Govinda Basumatary to open a channel of communication with the organisation's Bangladesh-based leadership. This resulted in a ceasefire agreement between NDFB and the Government on 25 May 2005. The agreement stated that the NDFB agree to cease hostile action against security forces and civilians. In return, the security forces would not carry out operations against the group's members. The agreement also stipulated that NDFB members would disarm and live in camps protected by the military for a year, and would refrain from assisting other militant groups. The pact came into force on 1 June 2005. However, certain factions of NDFB continued militancy.

NDFB (P), the pro-talks factions led by B Sungthagra supported peace talks with the governments. NDFB (R), led by Daimary, refused to give up militancy. In December 2008, the NDFB (P) indicated its plans to indirectly or directly participate the Lok Sabha elections. In 2012, I. K. Songbijit, the chief of the NDFB (R) faction's "Boroland Army", announced the formation of a nine-member "interim national council", resulting in a split. Amit Shah signed a historic peace treaty with factions on NDFB in February 2020.

CHAPTER XIII

Splits

After the <u>Operation All Clear</u> in 2003 the then united NDFB decided to go for ceasefire and talk to resolve the political issue in 2004. The proposal was submitted in 2008 and there was a meeting of the joint military council in Manipur. The secretary in the ministry of development of north east region, Naveen Verma, told the general secretary of the outfit that they must amend their proposition instead of negotiation at table or in other words they were forced to revise it, amend it and write a new memorandum.

There would have been no talks and extension of ceasefire unless the proposition was revised and amended which was submitted by the faction now known as <u>National Democratic Front of Boroland - Progressive</u> and the faction led by Ranjan Daimary who rejected it was then known as the Anti-Talks Faction, which further split into two factions.

NDFB have a sizeable number of sophisticated weapons including AK-series rifles. Since they have camps in Myanmar across Arunachal Pradesh, they have easy access to the latest weapons.

CHAPTER XIV

Activities

The group primarily operates in the region to the north and north-west of the Brahmaputra river. It is active in the Bongaigaon, Kokrajhar, Darrang, Barpeta, Dhubri, Nalbari and Sonitpur districts of Assam. It has also been active in the Garo Hills region of Meghalaya. It has used the neighbouring Bhutan as a refuge, crossing the border in the Manas National Park area. In December 2003, the Royal Bhutan Army initiated a crackdown on the group's activities in Bhutan.

CHAPTER XV

Disbanding

NDFB disbanded itself at two locations in accordance with a clause in Memorandum of Settlement (MoS) signed by the four factions and the other stakeholders with the Indian Government on 27 January 2020. While disbanding, the NDFB (P) leader Gobinda Basumatry said "To find a solution to political, economic, social and cultural issues of Bodo people, the Bodo Security Force was formed in 1986. It was renamed as NDFB in 1994. Our fight has finally come to an end after 34 years of armed struggle within and outside the country... from Nepal, Bangladesh, Myanmar and Bhutan. We believe that the NDFB movement has been a successful one and so we are disbanding the group."

CHAPTER XVI

Terrorism and its forms in the present scenario

Terrorism has no universal definition. Some people say that terrorism is a kind of violence related to politics, i.e. political violence. Others say that terrorism means creating fear in the minds of people. Some of the definitions by Indian scholars relates terrorism to gun culture.

However in most of the political science textbooks, terrorism has been defined as a threat to human security. Security generally means freedom from any kinds of threat. There are two notions of security, which are traditional security and non-traditional security. Traditional security comes from military threats to one country by another country. Non-Traditional security go beyond military threats to cover a wide range of threats which are affecting the conditions of human existence. Terrorism is rightly a non-traditional security.

Terrorism is a global and complex phenomenon. The meaning of terrorism is difficult to define because of its changing nature. Some people prefer to call it violence which others don't agree with the definition of terrorism as violence alone, since there are many incidents of silent attacks. Many scholars calls it a politically motivated violence which others again says that all terrorism are not politically motivated. In some countries of the world, terrorists attacks are more frequent. Terrorism is often regarded as a process in which the politics of many country revolves today.

In this age of the 21ˢᵗ century, terrorism has generally become a permanent process. Terrorism has taken its deep roots in the globe and its very hard to be eradicated. It has different kinds/forms/variants. Some people call it an artificial threat while others says that terrorism had its roots in the early state of nature.

CHAPTER XVII

Definition of Terrorism

Guptajit Pathak (2011) in his book "Politics in India since independence" has mentioned that the Assam Movement from 1979-85 is the best example of movement against the illegal immigrants. The Assamese people suspected that there were many illegal immigrant settlers from Bangladesh. They felt that unless these foreign nationals are detected and deported they would reduce the indigenous Assamese into a minority.

Parag Deka (2015) in his book "Contemporary Political Issues and Ideologies" has mentioned that the immigration process has helped in the development of the problems of insurgency in North East India. In some cases it has been found that the indigenous people resort to insurgency in the fear of losing their identity. The North East India has already witnessed several insurgency movement based on this migration issue.

Prashant Agarwal (2006) in his book "South Asia: Peace and Development" has mentioned that North East India as a region is a land lock in which different social groups belonging to various racialist origins have migrated from time to time through the history making the region itself into a conglomerate mass of inter-ethnic group interaction and ultimately leading to multi-ethnic, multi-lingual and multi-cultural region.

NamrataGoswami (2010) in her book "Bangladeshi Illegal Migration into Assam" has mentioned that the issue of Bangladeshi illegal migration has troubled the state of Assam for decades now. Assamese political and social discourses fear that this unchecked migration from across the border will subvert their way of life and change the demographic profile of the state in the near future.

N.C. Pathak (2014) in his book "Human Rights in India" mentioned that in the region of North East India; tensions come between the states and the central government as well as amongst the tribal people, who are natives of these states, and migrant peoples from other parts of India.

N.S. Narahani (2002) in his book "Security Threats to North East India" has mentioned that the earliest known migration was of Austeriods, and some Dravidians around 5000 B.C. These were the earliest known inhabitants. This was followed by waves of migrations of Mongoloid stocks from Southern China and Tibet. The progeny are the present day Bodos, Mishings, Raj Banshis, Akas, Daflas and Abors.

SanjibBaruah (2014) has highlighted the nation building in multi-ethnic policy to focus the insurgency in Assam.

Ajanta's Standard Dictionary defines terrorism as "government by terror or extreme fear."

Arab Convention for the Suppression of Terrorism defines terrorism as "any act or threat of violence, whatever its motives or purposes, that occurs in the advancement of an individual or collective criminal agenda and seeking to sow panic among people, causing fear by harming them, or placing their lives, liberty or security in danger, or seeking to cause damage to the environment or to public or private installations or property or to occupying or seizing them, or seeking to jeopardize a national resources."

Central Intelligence Agency (C.I.A.) has defined terrorism as the "threat or use of violence for political purposes when such action is intended to influence the attitude and behaviour of a target group other than its immediate victim and its ramifications transcend national boundaries."

Encyclopedia Britannica defines terrorism as "the calculated use of violence to create a general climate of fear in a population and thereby to bring about a particular political objective."

Encyclopaedia of Social Science has defined terrorism as a "term used to describe the method, or theory behind the method, whereby an organized group or party seeks to achieve its avowed aim through the systematic use of violence."

European Union (EU) law defines terrorist offences are acts committed with the aim of seriously intimidating a population and unduly compelling a government or international organization to perform or abstain from performing any act.

League of Nations Convention (1937) defines terrorist acts are "all criminal acts directed against a State and intended or calculated to create a state of terror in the minds of particular persons or a group of persons or the general public."

Merriam Webster Dictionary defines terrorism as "the systematic use of terror especially as a means of concern."

Oxford Dictionary defines terrorism as "the use of violent action in order to achieve political aims or to force a government to act."

United Nations General Assembly condemned terrorist acts by using the following political description of terrorism in 1994: criminal acts intended or calculated to provoke a state of terror in the general public, a group of persons or particular persons for political purposes are in any circumstance unjustifiable, whatever the considerations of a political, philosophical, ideological, racial, ethnic, religious or any other nature that may be invoked to justify them.

"Do not treat others in a manner that you would not like others to treat you." – Confucius

"When it comes to terrorism, we will do whatever is necessary to protect our Nation." – Donald John Trump

"Our enemy is a radical network of terrorists and every government that supports them." – George Walker Bush

Universal Definition of Terrorism

The United Nations has been trying for years to arrive at a satisfactory definition of terrorism. This has not been possible because of political differences and divergent perceptions among the different states. We are living in a world in which some states condemn terrorism, while states that use terrorism to govern or as an instrument of foreign policy often refuse to acknowledge their participation in terrorism. The debates that revolve round the application of terrorism and the value judgements that accompany the concept further increase the complexity of terrorism. Terrorism creates ethical dilemmas for individuals as well as nations because it combined the struggle for power and freedom, heroic self-sacrifice, with ruthless and callous disregard for human lives.

CHAPTER XVIII

Causes of Terrorism

Terrorism causes mainly because of the following reasons

i.   To force the government to fulfill their economic, political and social demands.

ii. Terrorists are basically paid for it by their group or organisation.

iii. To attrack the attention of the people of other countries and media.

iv. To make democracy ineffective because they do not have any faith in democracy.

CHAPTER XIX

Kinds of Terrorism

1. State Terrorism: State Terrorism (also called State Sponsored Terrorism) is a kind of terrorism which is supported by the state and the government. Examples of State Terrorism includes the acts like the black laws, secret killings, open killings and so on. In the year 2002, the Bush Administration in the United States has listed some states as rough states (axis of evil) which includes Iran, Iraq and North Korea. Moreover the Bush Administration has also stated that some of them have even developed Weapons of Mass Destruction.

1. Non State Terrorism: Non State Terrorism is a kind of terrorism which are run by the non state actors against the state and the government.

3. Social Terrorism: Social Terrorism (also called Social Evils) is a kind of terrorism which is supported by the society like witch hunting and kangaroo court trial. It is also related to the unethical use of social media.

4. Racial Terrorism: Racial Terrorism (also called Racial Discrimination or Caste Discrimination) is a kind of terrorism relating to varna (which means race or caste). It includes acts like the Apartheid.

5. Cyber Terrorism: Cyber Terrorism (also called Cyber Crime) is a type of crime or terrorism relating to the

internet. In other words, cyber means internet and cyber crimes means the crimes arising out of internet. Cyber Crimes are the most common problems of the world today. There are more and more uses of Internet and it has led to the increase in the number of Cyber Crimes. It involves the acts like hacking of governmental websites, bank fraudsters, cyber-bullying and so on.

6. International Terrorism: International Terrorism is a kind of terrorism which is operating worldwide. It targets the people of more than one country just like the 9/11 attacks.

7. Cross Border Terrorism: Cross Border Terrorism is a kind of terrorism when a person tries to infiltrate illegally into the territory of another country by allegedly crossing its border. It is prevalent in the Northern and North Eastern Region of India.

8. Economic Terrorism: Economic Terrorism (also called Financial Terrorism) is a kind of terrorism which attempts to destabilize the economy by different acts like printing and supplying of fake currency notes.

9. Narco Terrorism: Narco Terrorism is a kind of terrorism which is related to the use of narcotics or intoxicants. This kind of terrorism destroys the very basis of the state by creating addiction among its population to drugs, heroin, cocaine and the like.

10. Prison Terrorism: Prison Terrorism (also called Prison Riot) is an act of concerted defiance or disorder by a group of prisoners against the prison administrators,

prison officers or other group of prisoners.

11. Silent Terrorism: Silent Terrorism (also called Silent Attack or Silent Killer) is a kind of terrorism which attacks a person silently like poisoning and so on.

12. Neo Terrorism (New Terrorism) or Ultra Modern Terrorism: It is a very new kind of terrorism which includes any sources of threat. It includes theft, dacoity, robbery, acid attacks and so on. It also includes all other sources of terrorism which are not specifically classified yet like deforestation, illegal trade in wildlife and so on.

The use of violence for a particular purpose to change the status quo has failed in achieving its targets and thus new trends of terrorism have emerged. New terrorism is multi-purposely formed. New terrorism is indiscriminate in nature. While old terrorism attempts to attack only selected targets, new terrorism is always ready to use extreme indiscriminate violence at any moment. New terrorism is distinct in character, aiming at the destruction of the entire society and elimination of large sections of the population. New terrorism operates in a strong global network. According to new terrorism, the use of any kind of weapon like Weapons of Mass Destruction (WMD), Chemical, Biological, Radiological and Nuclear weapons (CBRN) is justifiable. No distinction is made between combatants and non-combatants. New terrorism exists only for conducting terrorist attack and does not get training and moral support from the state supporters. The organizational structure of new terrorism is flexible and less hierarchical. The members of terrorist groups can work independently within their areas so that they can adjust in any situation easily and also side by side maintains constant link with their higher authority. They maintain smooth communication by using information and communication technologies. New terrorism does not receive financial aids from the state backers rather their finance comes from drug trafficking, credit card fraud network, money laundering, legal business investment and donation.

New Terrorism has brought us back to the New State of Nature. Even though the organised state was created to get rid of the state of nature, terrorism has created chaos in contemporary era.

13. Ragging as a Terrorism: Ragging Terror or just ragging involves abuse, humiliation or harassment of new entrants or junior students by the senior students. It often takes a malignant form wherein the newcomers may be subjected to psychological or physical torture.

The scholars who defines terrorism as creating fear in the minds of the people often considers ragging as a part of terrorism since it create great fear psychosis in the minds of the people.

14. Environmental Terrorism: Environmental Terrorism consists of one or more unlawful actions that harm or destroy environmental resources or deprive others of their use. More colloquially, the phrase is also used to label actions seen as the unnecessary or unjustified destruction of the environment for personal or corporate gain.

15. Bio Terrorism: Bio Terrorism is a kind of terrorism which is mainly aimed at the destruction of living things

like plants, crops, animals, livestocks, humans and so on. It involves use of biological or chemical weapons like virus, bacteria and other germs.

CHAPTER XX

Consequences of Terrorism

i. Property of crores is being destroyed and destroyed by senseless people.

ii. Terrorists are creating great fear in the minds of the people.

iii. They sometimes attack religious places which causes communal riots and a large number of people are killed.

iv. The government has to spend huge amount of budget in providing training and modern equipment to the armed forces for the eradication of terrorism. If these money would have been used for constructive purposes, it can be used for providing healthcare and medical facilities to the people.

CHAPTER XXI

Difference between Insurgency and Terrorism

Often terrorism is confused with insurgency. There are, however, some major differences between terrorism and insurgency. Terrorism is usually the weapon of a small group, but insurgency enjoys a far great volume of mass support.

Because the terrorists constitute a small group, they do not try to establish control over any territory or run a government. Insurgents, on the other hand, try to replace the old regime with one of its own seeking. The endeavour of the insurgents is to enlarge and expand the base they will govern as models which will attract the population and convert them to their cause.

The term "Insurgency" and "Terrorism" has different meanings. The word Insurgency means Revolutionary who are fighting for their rights. Insurgents often enjoys support of the people. But the term Terrorism means working against humanity. Terrorists has no caste or religion. It just aims to cause harm or injury to others without any motive.

French historian Sophie Wahnich distinguishes between the revolutionary of the French Revolution and modern day terrorism and the 9/11 attacks. Sophie Wahnich has stated that Revolutionary is not Terrorism. To make a moral equivalence between the Revolution and September 2001 is historical and philosophical nonsense. The violence exercised on 11 September 2001 aimed neither at equality nor liberty.

CHAPTER XXII

Insurgency in North East India

In the North Eastern Region of India, there are many Indigenous groups who are enlisted in the category of Schedule Tribes. The first group to migrate in North East India are the Austro-Asiatic group of people who have migrated during the pre-historic period. The Austro-Asiatic groups of people includes the tribes like Khasis and Jaintias. They have migrated into the North East India during the pre-historic period, i.e. before recorded history.

The second group to migrate into the North East India are the Tibeto-Burman groups like Boros, Rabhas and Garos. They have migrated from the present day Tibet (China) and Burma (Myanmar). The Ahoms who ruled Assam from 1253 to 1826 is believed to have been migrated from Mong Mao in China. The followed the Brahmaputra river and accidentally reached Assam in 1228. In 1253, they established the Ahom Kingdom at Charaideo under the leadership of Sukapha. They ruled Assam till the signing of the Treaty of Yandaboo between the British and the Burmese in 1826. Sukapha was the founder and the first King of the Ahom Kingdom while PurandarSingha was the last King of the Ahom Kingdom. A total of about 40 Ahom Kings ruled Assam from 1253 to 1826. With the signing of the Treaty of Yandaboo between the British and the Burmese on 24th February 1826, Assam became a part of the British Empire.

In Assam, Indigenous People are those groups who have migrated before 1826. They are regarded as the sons of the soil.

At a certain period of time in history, almost all the indigenous people had their own Kingdom ruled by their own Kings and Queens under different dynasties. They have their own unique identity like language, culture, customs, traditions, beliefs and so on.

However with the advent of the British rule, most of the Kingdoms were incorporated into the British Empire one after another. At present, most of the Indigenous People are enlisted into the category of Scheduled Tribes by the Government of India.

Indigenous People in North East India are having their own unique identity like language, religion, culture, customs, traditions and so on. Tripura was once a Tribal majority state. The 1931 census of Tripura shows the Tribal population at more than 90 percent. When Tripura became a part of the Indian Union in 1949, the Tribal population in Tripura was still 70 percent. But in 1991, the non-tribal population in Tripura has gone up to 70 percent and the Tribal population was reduced to just 30 percent. The 2011 census of Tripura shows the non-tribal population at 90 percent while the Tribal population has become just 10 percent. The Indigenous People have been reduced to a microscopic minority in their own lands.

As a result of fear of losing their identity, we have seen several ethnic movements in North East India. Each and every tribe of North East India wanted to have their own separate homeland for the promotion, protection and preservation of their unique identity.

Most of the Indigenous People in the world today are facing an identity crisis. America originally belonged to the Red Indians. But today we have seen that the Red Indian population in America is nearly or equal to zero. Such is the case in other parts of the world too. The number of the

Indigenous People in the world have been decreasing day by day.

In the North East India, there are many different ethnic groups who have their own unique identity, language, culture, customs, traditions and so on. The North-East originally consists of seven states. And in this region, regional aspirations reached a turning point in the 1980s. This region is sorrounded by China, Myanmar, Bhutan, Bangladesh and Nepal. This region serves as India's gateway to South-East Asia. At present, Sikkim is also included along with these seven states. Therefore, instead of seven, it has eight states now.

This region has witnessed a lot of changes since 1947. Tripura, Manipur and Khasi Hills of Meghalaya were the princely states which merged with India after independence. North East India is conncctcd to the mainland India only by a 21 km long Siliguri corridor known as the "Chicken Neck". It is located in a geographically strategic location. Due to its geo-strategic location, North East India has special importance in India's Look East Policy.

There are generally three issues which are dominating the Politics of North East India:-

a. Demands for Regional Autonomy:- Ethnic Identity, language and region are the grounds on which people claim to have separate states.
b. Secessionist Movements:- There are some extreme groups who demands complete independence or separation from India.
c. Movement against the outsiders:- The Assam Movement from 1979 to 1985 is one of the best examples of movement against the outsiders. The Assamese

suspected that there were many illegal immigrants from Bangladesh. They felt that unless those foreign nationals are detected and deported, they would reduce the Indigenous People of Assam into a minority in their own lands. Assam Movement ended with the signing of the historic Assam Accord on 15th August 1985, but it did not solve the problems of the illegal immigration. The issue of illegal immigration still continues to be a dominating issue in the politics of Assam and other states of North East India.

All these issues have given rise to the problems of Insurgency in North East India.

In the North East India, several armed factions operate. All the seven states of North East India except Sikkim faces the problems of Insurgency.

CHAPTER XXIII

Insurgency in Assam

The United Liberation Front of Assam (ULFA) is said to be one of the most significant insurgent groups in Assam. ULFA was formed in April, 1979 with an aim to establish a Sovereign Assam through an armed struggle. The ULFA continued its activities in a violent way. At present ULFA has been divided into several factions led by Jiten Dutta, ArabindaRajkhowa and PareshBaruah. Jiten Dutta's faction is known as the Surrendered ULFA or SULFA. ArabindaRajkhowa's faction is known as pro-talks ULFA which is in negotiation with the Government. The faction led by PareshBaruah known as ULFA (Independent) is still running its insurgent activities with an aim to establish a Sovereign Assam.

The National Democratic Front of Bodoland which was active from 1986 to 2020 was formed with an aim to establish a Sovereign Bodoland. However the group surrendered with the establishment of the Bodoland Territorial Region.

CHAPTER XXIV

Insurgency in Manipur

Manipur was a princely state which was incorporated into the Indian Union on 15th October 1949 by an act called the Instrument of Accession. However after the Government of India occupied Manipur, there was quite anger and dissatisfaction among the Indigenous People of Manipur. This led to the proliferation of armed insurgent groups in Manipur. The United National Liberation Front (UNLF) which was founded in 1964 under the leadership of ArambamSamarendra Singh is the oldest Meitei insurgent group. It was formed with an aim to establish an Independent Socialist State of Manipur. Another insurgent group, the Peoples Liberation Army (PLA) was founded on 25th September 1978 under the leadership of N. Biseshwar Singh. It was also formed with an aim to liberate Manipur from India. At present, Manipur is considered to be the most violent state in North East India with a huge number of insurgent groups. India imposed the Armed Forces Special Powers Act (AFSPA) for the first time in Manipur in 1958. The current scenario in Manipur is uncertain with chaos, disorder and confusion. Both state as well as the non-state actors are responsible for creating trouble in Manipur.

CHAPTER XXV

Insurgency in Nagaland

The Nagas are considered to be the mother of all insurgencies in North East India. The Naga National Council (NNC) was the first group to dissent in 1947 and in 1956, they went underground. The NNC under the leadership of Z.A. Phizo declared independence of Nagaland on 14th August 1947.

In 1980, the National Socialist Council of Nagaland (NSCN) was formed as a result of condemning the Shillong Accord. The Shillong Accord was signed between the Government of India and the Naga Federal Government in which the Nagas decided to give up the demand for Sovereignty.

After the formation of NSCN in 1980, Insurgency in Nagaland got afresh. In 1988, NSCN was divided into two factions: NSCN (IM) led by IssacChisiSwu and TuingalengMuivah and NSCN (K) led by S.S. Khaplang.

However the Government of India is able to manage the NSCN (IM) in 1997 and NSCN (K) in 2000 for ceasefire. But due to the slow pace of negotiations and lacklustre attitude for finding permanent solution to the Naga problem, NSCN (K) abbrogates ceasefire and went underground once again in the year 2015.

NSCN (K) also joined hands with the ULFA (I), NDFB (S) and KLO to form the United National Liberation Front of Western South East Asia (UNLFWSEA) which is an umbrella organisation of different insurgent groups of North East India. The term Western South East Asia (WESEA) is used by the insurgent groups to describe the

North East India.

CHAPTER XXVI

Insurgency in Mizoram

After Independence, the Mizo Hills area was made an autonomous district within Assam. Some Mizos believed that they were never a part of British India and therefore did not belong to the Indian Union. But the movement for secession gained popular support after the Assam Government failed to respond adequately to the great famine of 1959 in the Mizo Hills. The Mizo's anger led to the formation of the Mizo National Front (MNF) under the leadership of Laldenga. The MNF fought a guerilla war, got support from the Pakistani Government and secured shelter in the then East Pakistan. The Indian Security Forces countered it with a series of repressive measures of which the common people were the victims. At the end of the two decades, Laldenga came back and started negotiations with the Government of India. Rajiv Gandhi steered these negotiations to a positive conclusion. In 1986, a peace agreement was signed between Rajiv Gandhi and Laldenga. As per this accord, Mizoram was granted full fledged statehood with special powers and the MNF agreed to give up secessionist struggle. Today, Mizoram is one of the most peaceful places in the North Eastern Region and has taken big strides in literacy and development. This accord proved a turning point in the history of Mizoram.

CHAPTER XXVII

Insurgency in Tripura

The insurgent tension in Tripura started in the end of 1970s due to the ethnic conflict between the immigrants and the Indigenous Tribal People. The Tripura Tribal Youth Federation (TTYF) is the main insurgent group of Tripura that was formed in 1967. Bijoy Kumar Hrangkhawl, the leader of the underground wing later formed the Tribal National Volunteers (TNV) and has become the main insurgent group of the state. After the surrender of Hrangkhawl in 1989, a new group within the organisation in the name of National Liberation Front of Tripura (NLFT) emerged as the most powerful insurgent group. Again, another group was formed as the All Tripura Tiger Force (ATTF) in 1990 to protect the interest of the native people of the land. Fortunately, due to the nexus between the political parties and insurgent groups make the region stable over the years.

CHAPTER XXVIII

Insurgency in Meghalaya

Meghalaya is a relative peaceful state in comparison to the other states of North East India. However, the problem of ethnic assertion arises due to certain reason such as division between tribal and non-tribal, identity crisis and corruption. The major insurgent groups are the Garo National Liberation Army (GNLA), Hynniewtrep National Liberation Council (HNLC) and the Achik National Volunteer Council (ANVC). The ANVC was formed under the leadership of Dilash R. Marak and Jerome Momin in 1995 with an aim of forming an Achik State in the Garo Hills.

The Hynniewtrep National Liberation Council (HNLC) was formed in 1992 with an aim to have a separate state from the Garo and other non-tribal of the region. This organisation represent the interest of the Khasi tribes.

The Garo National Liberation Army (GNLA) was formed in 2009 with an aim to establish a separate Garoland for the Garo people.

CHAPTER XXIX

Insurgency in Arunachal Pradesh

The Arunachal Dragon Force (ADF) was formed in 2001 to protect the ethnic identity and to have a sovereign state for the Khamti tribes. The ADF receive training and other form of support from the NSCN and the ULFA.

CHAPTER XXX

Conclusion

From the above discussion, we have come to know that **terrorism is any kind of threat from any thing to any other thing.** It may be threat from any sources be it living or non-living, animals or plants and so on. In this age of the 21st century, it has become a process. In some countries of the world, it has run parallely with politics. Politics generally means struggle for power. It generally means a healthy competition or struggle for power. But in the contemporary era the struggle for power has become unhealthy and destructive. During the Cold War era, there was a very dangerous arms race in the world. After the US dropped two atom bombs to defeat Japan, the different countries of the world thought that atom bomb was the monopoly of the US. Within a few yearsthe USSR also developed atomic weapons and it entered the field and challenged the hegemony of the US. This gave birth to a dangerous arms race in the world. The powerful nations tried to become more and more powerful and the nations which are not powerful also tried to develop weapons including nuclear weapons.

Even in national politics also, there developed an unhealthy competition for power. Terrorism is one kind of unhealthy struggle for power.

CHAPTER XXXI

Suggestion

1. Through the help of more education, rational and scientific outlook, we can stop terrorism.
2. Short term political or material benefit would encourage the terrorist.
3. Political knowledge should be given to the terrorist.
4. Government should help the terrorist through financially and by giving employment because most of the terrorist are educated persons.
5. Ethical knowledge should be given to the people.
6. Anti-Terrorism, Anti-Alien and Anti-Corruption Department must be set up in different institutions.